MW01241747

Made in the USA
Middletown, DE
03 August 2023

36177609R00064